BROOKLANDS COLLEGE LIBRARY
WEYBRIDGE, SURREY KT13 8TT

D0229835

ACCESSION NO. ....

CLASSIFICATION NO. 074745

745.2

TITLE Terence Conran—Design & the Quality

AUTHOR WILHIDE

DATE OF RETURN	DATE OF RETURN	DATE OF RETURN
07 MAY 2013		
16 APR 2013		
29. MAY 2002		
17. JAN 2002		
16. NOV 2000		
-2. NOV 2000		
-2 MAR 2000		
17. FEB 2000		
28. JAN 2000		
31. AUG. 1999		

This item must be returned on or before the last date
entered below.   Subject to certain conditions, the loan
period may be extended on application to the Librarian.

BROOKLANDS COLLEGE LIBRARY
HEATH ROAD, WEYBRIDGE, SURREY KT13 8TT
Tel: (01932) 797906

CUTTING EDGE

Terence Conran

ELIZABETH WILHIDE

Terence Conran

Design and the Quality of Life

THAMES AND HUDSON

First published in Great Britain
in 1999 by Thames and Hudson Ltd, London

Design copyright © 1999 The Ivy Press

Text copyright © 1999 The Ivy Press

Any copy of this book issued by the publisher is sold
subject to the condition that it shall not by way of
trade or otherwise be lent, resold, hired out or
otherwise circulated without the publisher's prior
consent in any form of binding or cover other than
that in which it is published and without a similar
condition including these words being imposed on
a subsequent purchaser

All Rights Reserved. No part of this publication may
be reproduced or transmitted, in any form or by any
means, electronic or mechanical, including photocopy,
recording or any other information storage and
retrieval system, without prior permission in writing
from the publisher

British Library Cataloguing-in-Publication Data

A catalogue record for this book is
available from the British Library

ISBN 0-500-01918-5

Originated and printed by Hong Kong Graphic,
Hong Kong

Contents

'**M**y belief is simply that if reasonable and intelligent people are offered something that is well made, well designed, of a decent quality and at a price they can afford, then they will like it and buy it. This is the abiding principle to which I hold, whether as a designer, retailer or restaurateur. I've designed literally hundreds of thousands of things, but hardly anyone ever notices them. They tend not to be design icons as such, but are often rather more mundane – designs that involve changing the colour or edge of a plate, or the handle of something, so that it just slips into life...'

Terence Conran

Introduction

SOUTH OF THE THAMES, running east from Tower Bridge along the waterfront, is a London landmark in the making. On the ground level of the converted warehouses of Butlers Wharf a cluster of food shops and restaurants bustles with City workers extending their lunch hours or lingering in the evening over steak and kidney puddings, plateaux de fruits de mer and the spectacular view. This is Terence Conran's 'Gastrodrome'.

Half a block further along the river walk is an attraction of a different kind. The pristine modernist frontage of the Design Museum rises like the prow of a ship at moorings: it is home to the only permanent collection of twentieth-century design in Britain, to the Conran Foundation's annual selection of innovative new work and to a programme of provocative exhibitions, attractions that draw a steady stream of students, schoolchildren and the culturally curious.

Venture still further along Shad Thames, past Victorian warehouses named after the spices that were once traded here, and you will reach a striking contemporary building of concrete, glass and steel designed by one of Britain's leading architects, Michael Hopkins. Large plate glass windows on the ground floor display the clean modern lines of sofas and chairs, tables and storage units, all with an unmistakable stamp of quality. Above this showroom for Conran Contracts (which supplies furniture to offices, hotels and restaurants) are several floors of offices, the creative hub of the many Conran design businesses, shops and restaurants. And at the very top, its roof terrace luxuriant with container-grown plants, is the apartment which is Terence Conran's London home.

Living above the shop (alongside the restaurants, museum, offices and studios) is not a choice based on simple expediency, but is entirely symptomatic of Conran's philosophy of design. Terence Conran, more than any other figure in post-war Britain, has revolutionized the way ordinary people shop, eat and live. His mission has been to 'open people's eyes' – to their surroundings, to the everyday objects they use, to the food on their plates, to the spaces inside and outside their homes. Design, for Conran, is not an elitist activity or a theoretical exercise to be pursued in ivory towers, but is embedded in the choices of the real world. It is teapots that pour properly as much as architectural monuments, chairs that are comfortable to sit in as much as cult objects, restaurants that are alive with the buzz of people enjoying themselves as much as designer labels.

Butlers Wharf, with its Gastrodrome and Design Museum, is but one example of the integrated nature of Conran's approach. There are many others. The Conran Shop, first opened in 1973, now occupies the lower floors of the Michelin Building in London's Fulham Road, which was rescued and renovated by Conran in partnership with his architects in 1987. You can buy furniture there – or flowers from the forecourt stall. You can eat

'I've always viewed the process of design from the perspective of how something is going to be made, rather than designing it in the abstract and getting someone else to add the detail.'

Conran's integrated approach to design is seen clearly at Butlers Wharf, shown here looking west with Butlers Wharf Chop House in the foreground.

lunch at the counter in the Oyster Bar – or dine upstairs at Bibendum, consistently rated one of London's top five restaurants. Down the road it is a similar story. The former Bluebird garage on King's Road has been converted into a food-lover's paradise, with a huge fresh food market, furniture shop, flower market, restaurant, café and private dining club. Meanwhile at Barton Court in Berkshire, Conran's country house where he spends most weekends, converted farm buildings house the workshops of Benchmark, the company set up by Conran and Sean Sutcliffe, which now makes most of the furniture for Conran restaurants as well as many designs sold in the Conran shops worldwide.

Shops where you can eat, restaurants where you can buy a bunch of flowers or the ingredients for supper, homes where creative work takes place – it is small wonder that Conran's career resists hard and fast categorization. People still try. For those who remember the 1960s, there is the Conran of Habitat, the groundbreaking store that introduced the whole concept of 'lifestyle' shopping to post-war Britain, as well as such alien Continental imports as the garlic press and the duvet. Or there is Conran the entrepreneur, chairman of the Storehouse Group, the 1980s retailing empire which pioneered a radical redefinition of the British high street. More recently, there is Conran the restaurateur, whose ever-growing roster of eateries includes Bluebird, Bibendum, Quaglino's, Mezzo, Sartoria and the Coq d'Argent.

In the popular press, Conran is often (and somewhat to his irritation) known by the shorthand 'design guru', in recognition of his unofficial role as an arbiter of modern British taste.

It may be tempting to define Conran's career in terms of self-contained epochs, or simplistic labels, but the truth is that all of these interests and spheres of activity – design, food, business, writing, making things – have coexisted from the start. Conran opened his first café in 1953, a year after he set up his own furniture-making business and 11 years before the first Habitat. In 1956 he founded the Conran Design Group, which eventually grew to be one of the largest consultancies in Europe. Right from the beginning, Conran has always had designs on the way we live.

Beginnings

Terence Conran was born in 1931 and educated at Bryanston School in Dorset and the Central School of Arts and Crafts in London, where he studied textile design. Both institutions placed considerable importance on craftsmanship. At Bryanston, the key influence on Conran's development was Don Potter, an inspirational teacher of sculpture, pottery and metalwork who was himself taught by Eric Gill and Bernard Leach. At Central, Conran was much influenced by the sculptor Eduardo Paolozzi, with whom he later shared a welding workshop. To this day, craftsmanship remains integral to Conran's working methods: 'I've

Living above the shop: Terence Conran's London apartment at Butlers Wharf is located at the top of a building designed by leading British architect Michael Hopkins.

always viewed the process of design from the perspective of how something is going to be made, rather than designing it in the abstract and getting someone else to add the detail which allows it to be made,' he says.

Conran's reputation and sheer visibility as a businessman, whether as a hugely successful retailer or as a restaurateur, has occasionally eclipsed his role as a designer. 'People often ask me: "Do you still design?"', he says. 'But the only reason I am in business is to be able to do things and make things happen.' With the launch of Conran and Company in 1952, when he was only 21, he proceeded to make things happen. Conran had already been selling his own textile designs for four years; his first job after college was to mount an exhibition and produce a magazine for the newly formed Rayon Design Council; and his own work had been displayed at the Festival of Britain in 1951. After the launch of his company, his designs were spotted by Natasha Kroll, design manager of Simpson of Piccadilly, and he was invited to show his work at the store, designs which included a woven basket chair on three legs and a terracotta pot on a metal stand. He was understandably delighted when both Picasso and Philip Johnson bought his chairs – a great boost to his confidence at a time when he was 'finding it hard to pay the gas bill'.

Then in 1953 came an experience which amounted to a personal epiphany. Accompanied by photographer Michael Wickham, Conran visited France for the first time. In the early 1950s London was still emerging from wartime austerity; materials were in short supply, some food was still rationed, and decent, affordable places to eat were few and far between. France, particularly rural France, with its markets full of abundant fresh produce, its cafés and its restaurants, made a huge impact on Conran, who was smitten by the easy sensuality of everyday French living and the simple honesty and quality of ordinary goods such as pots and pans, tumblers and crockery piled high in local shops.

After a short stint working as a *plongeur* or washing-up boy in a Paris restaurant, Conran had been bitten by another bug. In characteristic fashion, he wasted little time putting his new enthusiasm into practice. The Soup Kitchen, opened in 1953 in Chandos Place, London, was Conran's first restaurant, serving simple meals of soup, bread and espresso coffee. The food was cheap and basic, but of good quality; the interior, with Conran furniture, vibrant colour and Fornasetti-style blown-up prints, set out to appeal to the young and fashion-conscious. This use of design to create a wholly integrated effect is an early example of what would become typical of Conran's subsequent work.

More restaurants and business enterprises followed, notably the Conran Design Group (founded in 1956), which rapidly grew into a multi-disciplinary practice designing graphics, packaging, products, shop interiors and exhibition displays. In the

The Bluebird Restaurant in King's Road forms part of a 'Gastrodrome' that includes a large foodmarket.

Fine cuisine from Quaglino's.

Food doesn't come much fresher than this: the Bibendum Oyster Van at Michelin House, Fulham Road.

10

early 1960s, the Design Group was responsible for one of the first corporate-identity reviews in Britain, for the sherry producer Harvey's of Bristol, a three-year programme that involved the design of shops and off-licences, packaging, liveries and a restaurant. A manual was produced to instruct the staff on the implementation of the new brand identity.

By the early 1960s, Conran was becoming identifiable with a particular aesthetic. A robust and simple modernity, the use of natural finishes and materials, colourful and graphic patterning, the sympathetic blend of old and new and a meticulous attention to detail characterized all his work, from shop and restaurant interiors to furniture and furnishings. With the creative side of the business now under one roof in Hanway Place off London's Tottenham Court Road, and a new furniture-making factory, opened in 1962, at Thetford in Norfolk, all the elements for Conran's future development were in place.

Habitat

The opening of Habitat in the Fulham Road in 1964 was a defining moment in contemporary British life. In retrospect, the timing could not have been more fortuitous. The Beatles were in the charts, London was swinging as never before and newspaper colour supplements, with their features on cookery, travel and fashion, had begun to chronicle the modern lifestyle. What could be guaranteed to be more of a hit than a chic new home furnishings shop located right in the heart of Chelsea?

But to see Habitat's success as inevitable is to severely underestimate both its groundbreaking originality and the major risks involved in its launch: Conran was by no means pushing at an open door. Furthermore, he was only just beginning to break into the domestic market; up to this point the bulk of his sales had been to the contract market. 'Opening Habitat was a very difficult decision,' he says. 'There was the danger that I might be accused by retailers of being in competition and hence they might have decided not to buy my furniture, which would have meant my lifelines would have collapsed.' Set against this risk, however, was the considerable frustration that Conran continued to experience in getting his products sold and marketed the way he wanted. Most furniture stores and departments still had all the visual appeal of a suburban front room, waiting lists for orders were long, and buyers' tastes remained profoundly conservative.

Conran's genius was to identify what the up-and-coming market of young middle-class customers wanted, and to offer it to them in an exciting and irresistible way. 'I never thought Habitat would ever be more than one shop, demonstrating a different way of selling furniture,' he says. In fact, it turned out to become much more than that, exemplifying the entire modern style of life – informal, energetic and adventurous.

'I never thought Habitat would ever be more than one shop, demonstrating a different way of selling furniture.'

The first Habitat catalogue, introducing the store's carefully selected range of household products and furnishings, ushered in an entirely new concept of shopping for the home.

11

Habitat was bursting with new products. The core merchandise was flat-pack furniture – Conran correctly predicted that customers would find the immediacy of taking purchases home well worth the small trouble of self-assembly. But most people buy large pieces of furniture fairly infrequently, so there were also smaller-scale products – glasses, pans, plates, cups, lampshades, tea towels and cushions – which were designed or sourced by Conran and his small team of buyers. Good quality, competitively priced and stacked high, just as Conran had seen goods on sale in France, such items also served to create the 'busy shop' atmosphere that kept people coming back time and again. 'Habitat's kitchen department was as significant as the furniture,' says Conran. 'It made these types of goods accessible for the first time.'

From the lower-case typography of the logo, to the carefully arranged room sets that suggested how furniture could be used, to the accompanying catalogue (recently listed by the *Sunday Telegraph* as one of the 'Ten Books That Changed Your Life'), Habitat was the first shop to identify its image and products as part of a wider ethos. It was an immediate success with the public and in the press; eventually it would prove a financial one.

Expansion

For the next two decades, Conran's expanding retail empire provided him with a widening arena for the exercise of his talents, both as a designer and as a 'chooser' of design. The 'editorial' role of selection – the 'one pair of eyes' that gives unity to all his enterprises – has proved one of his greatest strengths. Conran remembers directional meetings at Habitat, where he and his buyers debated coming trends and argued the virtues of new products, as 'among the most stimulating of my life'. 'An awful lot of what I do with buyers concerns direction,' he says. 'It comes from the gut and the brain, from seeing a huge amount of things and sensing what people don't have but might want if they were offered.' For Conran, one of the keys to retailing is for buyers 'not to work only from history, but from anticipation.'

Habitat grew rapidly and eventually expanded into Europe; in 1973, the first Conran Shop opened on Habitat's original site, born partially out of frustration at having to reject products for Habitat because they were too expensive, too esoteric or in limited supply. By the mid-1980s, Conran's impact on the high street was sealed with his chairmanship of Storehouse, a group which included, as well as Habitat, the Mothercare chain, British Home Stores, Heal and Son, Blazer, Richard Shops and FNAC. Here the challenge was 'to put a fresh cheerful face' on a huge range of products aimed at the ordinary high street customer. The Mothercare makeover, with its 'sweet pea' colours on packaging and graphics, established a winning new identity for what had been a very tired chain and anticipated new products and designs

Dining on an impressive scale: Mezzo, in London's Soho, seats 700 people on two floors.

'I have a taste for finding old property and converting it, and I have gained great satisfaction from bringing new life to areas of London which were formerly rather moribund.'

in the pipeline. Dowdy British Home Stores' repackaging as Bhs was similarly stage-managed in a design coup d'etat that featured in-store banners, a new fascia and a newly contracted name. Unfortunately, Conran's ambition to transform the high street stalwart into a British version of The Gap was ultimately frustrated. But he had the considerable satisfaction of seeing Next, a new chain of women's clothing stores based on market analysis and creative ideas from Conran Design Group, leap to success.

Meanwhile, Conran Design Group's list of clients grew to include some of the best-known international companies – from Ford Motors and Rank Xerox to ICI, Levi's and Sony. Prestigious projects ranged from the design of airport termini at Heathrow and Gatwick to the interior of the Land Rover 'Discovery'. Conran Roche, architects and town planners, founded in 1980, were responsible for many high-profile and award-winning buildings in Britain and Europe, both new and converted. 'I have a taste for finding old property and converting it,' says Conran, 'and I have gained great satisfaction from bringing new life to areas of London which were formerly rather moribund.'

New challenges

Conran's 'new life' began in 1990, after his resignation from Storehouse and the group's subsequent break-up. 'I've been happiest in the last eight to nine years, rebuilding the business with people I like,' he says. There are new Conran Shops in London and around the world, and a range of restaurants bringing the Conran touch to a whole new area of living.

Conran's approach to design is the natural expression of somewhat paradoxical qualities. Aesthetically, he has a taste for simplicity – basic forms, lack of clutter, the unpretentious (one of his favourite words is 'gutsy') – but at the same time, he has a sensualist's delight in quality – good food and wine, cigars, the patina of finish, the pattern of wood grain, the nap of fabric. Added to which he is a notorious perfectionist, with a rigorous eye for defects in function or appearance. He has the successful retailer's sixth sense, the ability to sniff the air and anticipate the coming mood, but he eschews novelty for the sake of it. He has a craftsman's love of materials and tools, but a manufacturer's practical concern for economy and efficiency.

Most important, against the tide of British culture which at times has seemed gridlocked in tradition, he has maintained a modernist's conviction that design has the power to improve people's daily lives. 'In no time in the history of any nation has taste changed so radically as it has in this country between the 1960s and 1990s. Part of this change is that more people are prepared to question things and think about whether they could be improved.' Conran's unique contribution has been to demonstrate the essential connection between design and the quality of life.

Terence Conran is always looking for new challenges. His renovation of Hotel Das Triest in Vienna (with CD Partnership) opened in 1996, and further hotel projects are under way.

'FORM FOLLOWS FUNCTION', the modernists' mantra, is for Conran not so much a theoretical position as robust common sense. 'Because of my upbringing in the crafts, and my experiences as a war child trying to achieve things in very difficult circumstances, I have always seen design from the point of view of "how are you going to make it?" ' he says. 'All my life I've had the knowledge that comes from having physically used my hands to make things. It all starts with a technique, or the quality of a material, and design decisions are made because I know how a certain material will behave or how a certain machine can be used efficiently or economically.'

As an early influence, Conran often cites his mother Christina, with her 'intense interest' in her children's aesthetic education. The best birthday present he can remember was 'a big sack of timber offcuts, nails and a hammer', an enlightened gift to a child more absorbed than most by the process of making things. Not only making, but also trading: during the lean war years, Conran's model ships and trains proved valuable items to be bartered (characteristically for more tools and materials), as well as playthings with which he and his sister Priscilla could amuse themselves.

'I find it intensely frustrating to see designers coming out of college who don't know how things work,' says Conran. 'My background in crafts and in manufacturing has been very influential in my work both as a designer and retailer. So many designers come up with a prototype and then expect the manufacturer to sort out how it will work. But I've always wanted to retain that ability.'

Conran's experience as a retailer has given him a keen awareness of the importance of price, which is another aspect often overlooked

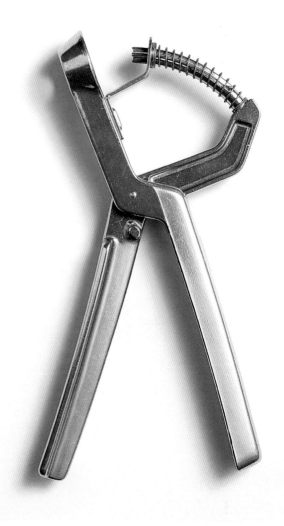

KITCHEN UTENSILS
The Conran Shop

Conran has an eye for well-made, simple products – from wooden spoons to lemon zesters and olive-stoners – whose form is a perfect expression of their function.

objects that simply do not work properly, whether these are pens that leak, tables with wobbly legs or fabrics that fall apart in the wash – or kitchens that are badly laid out. Pleasure in use remains just as important as visual delight, and he has little time for anything that seduces the eye but proves frustrating or disappointing in practice.

Conran's craft-based background places him in the English tradition of design that has descended from William Morris, design which is wholly integrated in the process of making. Unlike some of the more Luddite disciples of the Arts and Crafts movement, however, Conran has a fundamental respect for machines and what they can do. His early espousal of flat-pack designs, for example, may have satisfied Habitat customers' desire for immediacy, but it also represented an efficiency and precision of manufacture, and hence an economy of price.

One of Conran's great pleasures of recent years has been the establishment of Benchmark, the furniture-making business he founded with Sean Sutcliffe, and its growing sophistication as a producer of high-quality contemporary designs. The company has recently acquired one of the most advanced computer-controlled woodworking machines, a CNC router, which is able to perform highly intricate tasks with incredible ease and rapidity. With an amused irony, Conran points out that the same type of machine was used to recreate the carving during the restoration of Windsor Castle – not something that he expects his machine to emulate, however.

Benchmark's inevitable spoilage is quantities of timber offcuts. Conran, who hates to waste anything, found himself 'staring at piles of these offcuts and wondering if we couldn't make something out of them so they wouldn't end up on the fire'. Benchmark now sells a range of chopping boards, bookends, photo frames and door wedges – all highly functional, of course.

OFFCUT PRODUCTS
Benchmark Woodworking, 1998

Based at Barton Court, Conran's Berkshire home, Benchmark has a growing reputation as a producer of high-quality contemporary furniture. Offcuts are usefully turned into products such as chopping blocks and door wedges.

SWALLOWTAIL
Armchair, Conran
Collection 1997

With its compact, dynamic shape tapering to the flared line of the back, the Swallowtail is a tailored alternative to the squashy, rumpled easy chair. As with all Conran designs, the process begins with sketches on paper which are then worked up to sectional drawings, scale models and a full-size sample.

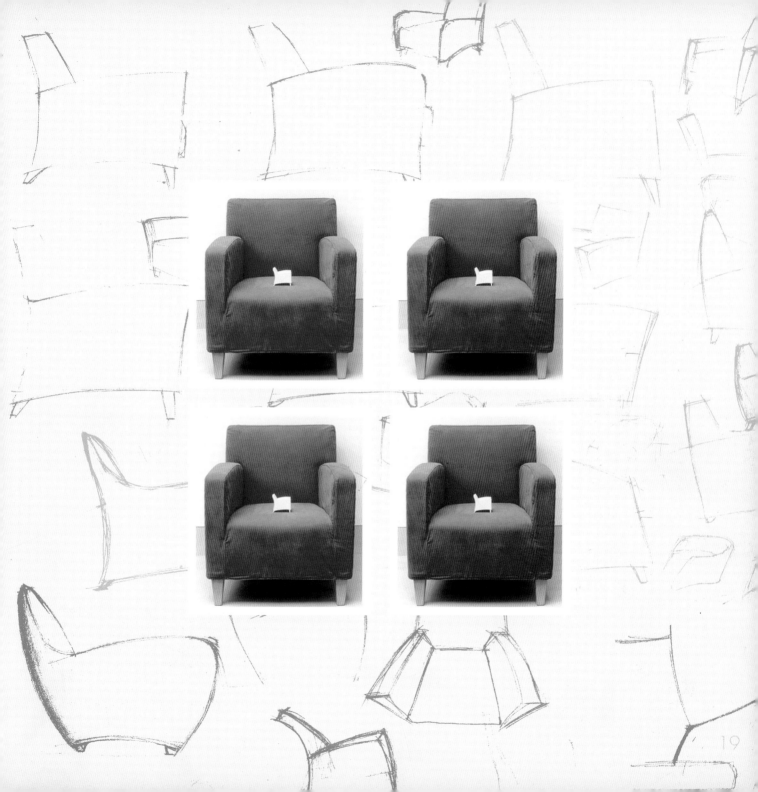

FURNITURE AND FITTINGS
Benchmark Woodworking, 1990s

Benchmark produces much of the furniture and fittings for Conran's restaurants, as well as products for his shops, all distinguished by Conran's appreciation of craftsmanship and materials. *Right:* **detail of tables for Bluebird Club bar.** *Clockwise from top left:* **selection of tables; 'Mosquito' console; club chairs and waiter station at Bluebird Club; Bluebird restaurant furnishings.**

MATERIAL QUALITY is inseparable from the process of making: they are flip sides of the same coin. Just as the plasticity of clay shapes what you can do with it, the characteristics of any material have a bearing on design – or should have. 'People don't always consider the selection of materials as part of the design process,' says Conran. Naturally enough, given his appreciation of different manufacturing techniques, he could hardly be accused of such an oversight.

During the Habitat years, the material with which Conran was most closely identified in the public's mind was pine. 'Never stripped pine,' he adds with some vehemence, correcting a particularly persistent popular misconception. 'In the 1950s and 60s pine was a very nice and very cheap material, and we often used it natural or stained. If you want a natural finish, the wood has to be perfect, with no sapwood.' Staining pine, oak and ash was a way of covering up the wood's natural imperfections and meant that Conran could produce his furniture more economically. 'We were also one of the first businesses in the country to make teak furniture. Obviously we were influenced by the Scandinavians, but we also used it because teak is very stable and does not expand and contract as much as other woods, and so jointing is less difficult.'

ALTO
Beech chopping boards, Conran Collection, 1997

For Conran, true quality, rather than spurious luxury, resides in an appropriate and generous use of materials.

CASPER
White porcelain, Conran Collection, 1997

The rolled rim of this simple white porcelain range makes the pieces less susceptible to chipping.

ZEUZERA
Rug, Conran Collection, 1997

Floor-level art: each rug begins as a painting by a Conran studio designer.

The role of design, in this material sense, performs the function of reconciling the desire for authenticity and integrity with the need to keep products affordable. A similar example also dates from the early Habitat period when Conran started selling jugs, coffee pots and mugs made of vitreous enamel. Vitreous enamelling was an exceptionally inexpensive process, but the products always had an old-fashioned, rather institutional feel. Instead, Conran added bright colour, a simple transformation that made a basically authentic material much more desirable. Flat-weave Indian dhurries were another Habitat find, but it was not simply a case of sourcing the goods and importing them. Conran and his buyers worked in collaboration with local carpet-makers to come up with fresh-looking designs that would sell in the European market. The results were very economical floor coverings made of a natural material, which also had a great contemporary appeal. More recently, Conran has been using zinc, another cheap material, on furniture, as much for its ability to acquire what he calls 'a patina of usage' as for its sharp modern aesthetic.

The integrity of materials matters a great deal to Conran, a concern that leads him to prefer the natural to the artificial or synthetic.

DJANGO
Japanese stoneware,
Conran Collection,
1997

Conran takes care to source the best materials and craftsmen for his products. This range of stoneware, produced in four colours, is made by a small family-run pottery in Nagoya, Japan.

SARTORIA
Restaurant and bar,
opened 1998

The subtle interplay of
materials – marble floor,
walnut bar and plywood
chairs – provides an
elegantly understated sense
of sophistication. Sartoria
is located in London's
traditional tailoring district,
a context acknowledged in
the choice of grey suiting as
sofa coverings.

He particularly loathes the inability of most synthetic materials to age with any grace: 'They are at their absolute best on day one and go rapidly downhill thereafter.' In part, this is Conran's dislike of false economy and spurious convenience, but it is also a distaste for the dishonesty of simulation. Natural materials, such as wood, cotton, linen, stone, steel, bronze and terracotta, have the capacity to mellow with time and acquire the depth of character that comes from careful use. Synthetics, on the other hand, are essentially something of a con, whose lookalike qualities can be literally skin-deep.

This is not to say that Conran has never designed anything in an artificial material. Back in the early 1970s, Airfix Plastics commissioned the Design Group to come up with a new range of products. 'We wanted to give plastic a feeling of quality by using it in a chunky fashion that would be like the solidity of old Bakelite,' recalls Conran. The 21 brightly coloured items of the 'Crayonne' range sold in large quantities both in Habitat and in other shops, and were chosen by the Museum of Modern Art in New York as an example of how attitudes to a material could be changed through design. Unfortunately, as Conran points out, plastic's great virtue, its economy, evaporated overnight in the wake of the oil crisis that followed the Arab–Israeli conflict.

SARTORIA
Restaurant and bar, opened 1998

Natural materials that age well and develop a pleasing patina with careful use have an innate integrity. Here the careful orchestration of soft and hard surfaces – marble and carpet, leather and linen – adds depth and character. The cutting pattern for Rex Harrison's suit hung on the wall of the restaurant *(top)* is another gentle nod at the area's tailoring tradition.

CRUSTACEA BAR
Bluebird restaurant,
opened 1997

The angled mirrors forming the backdrop to the crustacea bar – or 'altar' – add to the sense of visual plenty. This quality of simple abundance is one that Conran is always keen to promote in both his restaurants and his shop displays.

FRESH FOOD DISPLAYS
Bluebird Foodstore,
opened 1997

Conran's latest 'Gastrodrome', Bluebird, encompasses a large foodmarket selling fresh, seasonal produce as well as a restaurant, bar, café and club.

GLASS
Antique glass in Conran's apartment.
'Amonite' and 'Lutea' vases, Conran Collection, 1997

Conran has a particular fondness for glass and has collected pieces all his life, some of which are displayed in the entrance hallway of his London apartment (above). Handmade studio vases and bowls produced for the Conran Collection make a luminous display (right).

While Conran views materials with the practical eye of both a craftsman/manufacturer and a retailer, he also has an instinctive response to their sensual qualities. The way things feel, sound and smell provides another way of anchoring design ideas in the real world. He takes especial pleasure from the fact that the enticing aroma of the Conran Shops derives from the products themselves and is not the result of some cynical marketing ploy with synthetic scents dispersed at key locations. Authenticity is no less important when it comes to food. The freshness of ingredients, which are as unadulterated as possible, provides the basic integrity of the cooking in his restaurants, whatever the style of cuisine. As a retailer, of course, Conran is not unaware of the appetizing appeal of a seafood counter or a market stall.

Of all materials, glass is perhaps his personal passion and he has long been a collector, particularly of eighteenth-century pieces. Fragile, simple, with the idiosyncratic imperfections that are the mark of hand-making, such objects encapsulate his particular sense of material quality.

**The quality of everyday
life in France has been
an enduring influence
on Conran's approach
as a designer, retailer
and restaurateur.**

DESPITE A LONG HISTORY of invention and innovation, and a tradition of superb craftsmanship, an almost perverse indifference to the art of living has been a persistent characteristic of the British – something of a national blindspot. Suspicion of any foreign influence, the inhibition of class-consciousness and an 'I-haven't-tried-it-but-I-know-I-don't-like-it' mentality lingered long into the post-war era. But if ordinary British people are now more aware of what they've been missing and appear increasingly keen to make up for lost time, to a significant degree they have Conran to thank.

Conran is a fervent believer in design as something that 'adds value' to life and enhances enjoyment on an everyday level. His impact on British culture, as a designer, retailer and restaurateur, has been to persuade people that it is alright to enjoy themselves a little more. Holidays abroad and media exposure to a vast range of alternatives have gradually opened people's eyes to different ways of doing things, choices that Conran has been offering ever since the launch of Habitat over 30 years ago.

'How other cultures behave and what they do has been a very important influence on me,' he says. 'Part of the designer's role is to look for things to stock in the mind, like a databank, for possible use later on. I travel a lot, read lots of magazines and look at what other people have done, both old and new. Something will click – a plate of food, lighting, an arrangement of objects will trigger an idea. I might see a picture of a lobster with vivid red antennae against a mottled purple shell and think about using the same colours on a sofa...'

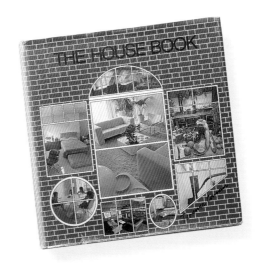

THE HOUSE BOOK
Published 1974

Packed with practical information and visual inspiration, *The House Book* began as an in-house training manual for Habitat staff, but grew to be one of the best-selling home design manuals of all time.

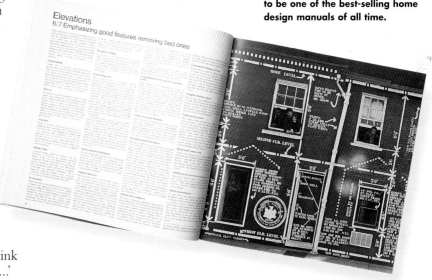

29

CRUSTACEA
BAR AND
STAIRCASE
Quaglino's, opened
1993
CIGARETTE
GIRL
Mezzo, opened
1995

Theatricality creates a sense of excited anticipation, vital for the success of a restaurant. Conran revived the glamour of Quaglino's, a glittering nightspot in the 1930s, with features such as the sweeping entrance staircase and mosaic crustacea bar.

ASHTRAY AND SALT
AND PEPPER PINCH
Quaglino's, 1993

The calligraphic flourish of the letter 'Q', translated into ashtrays or cruets, adds a touch of drama to the tabletop.

Ever since his early trips to France, Conran has been trying to promote that very French sense of easy informality, the blurring of indoors and out, the conviviality of street markets and courtyards, and relaxed sense of modernity, all of which may be expressed in products or environments but actually add up to an entire way of life. Habitat is generally credited as the first 'lifestyle' shop in Britain. Unlike other retail outlets at the time, which stocked a range of brands, Habitat itself became a brand, the act of selection implicit in the act of walking through the door. What was also implicit was the identification with a particular attitude to living. This was further reinforced by enterprises such as *The House Book* (published by Conran in 1974), which began life as an in-house training manual for Habitat staff but grew into an enormously popular style guide to planning, designing and equipping the home.

Shops that looked more like homes were one way of getting the message across. Today, restaurants increasingly offer the same potential for cross-referencing, as people attempt to recreate in their own kitchens the food they have enjoyed eating out, and adopt catering-style equipment and appliances to give an edge of professionalism to their endeavours. The influence cuts both ways. Restaurants such as the Pont de la Tour, with its street windows providing views of the kitchen in full swing, or Mezzo, with its dramatic double-height glazed partition providing diners with the spectacle of kitchen choreography, display Conran's desire to bring down the barriers.

But restaurants are also about creating a theatrical experience, and Conran's sense of stagecraft is used to set the scene for that excited anticipation – or 'buzz', in his words – of a roomful of people enjoying themselves. Described by Egon Ronay as 'an epoch-making restaurant', Quaglino's opened in 1993 after a two-year programme of design and building work. It had been a famous and fashionable haunt in the 1930s; its rebirth as a glamorous brasserie included a few nods and winks at its glittering past. 'I was watching an old Busby Berkeley movie and there was a cigarette girl and I thought "why don't we do that today?"' Quaglino's cigarette girls, sweeping entrance staircase and altar-like seafood bar tiled in luminous mosaic are pure drama, the height of an overall effect which is suitably scaled for a restaurant that serves over 1,000 people a day.

THE CONRAN SHOP
Michelin Building, Fulham Road,
opened 1987

**For Conran, successful retailing depends a
great deal on detail. His shops employ
clever juxtapositions to suggest how goods
will work in the home.**

The art of living can also be conveyed by creating a destination with a life of its own. 'In the plans for the Butlers Wharf development we took enormous trouble to make it mixed-use, a real regeneration of the South Bank, but unfortunately those dreams have not been realized to the extent I had hoped.' Bluebird, on the other hand, which Conran rates as 'one of the single most satisfying projects to date', has successfully created 'a little street or village courtyard atmosphere' that bubbles with activity. A similar potential is offered by the new Bridgemarket redevelopment in Manhattan's Upper East Side.

The same sensitivity to place influences Conran's approach to garden design. Conran is fond of quoting Sir John Soane's advice on the importance of 'hazard and surprise' in design. In horticultural terms, this means gardens that cannot be immediately grasped from a single viewpoint, but give up their secrets slowly as one moves through them. Then there is the influence of France and the desire to promote a closer integration of indoor and outdoor areas, so that the easy informality of outdoor living may transfer to the way one lives indoors. Most typically, Conran's own gardens in Berkshire and Provence are productive places where much of the fresh food for the houses is grown.

One of Conran's exciting new commissions is to redesign the interior of Concorde, a challenge with particular resonance for Conran since the aircraft is one of his favourite designs. Where will he begin? 'I intend to pull back from the memory bank all those images of luxury and quality and take it from there,' he says. No doubt the final design will encapsulate, in a small space, the art of living.

GARDEN AT BARTON COURT
Kintbury, Berkshire

When Conran acquired this eighteenth-century house and its 20 acres of grounds in 1972, both were in a derelict condition. The garden has been designed in the form of a series of interconnected outdoor 'rooms', and includes a highly productive kitchen garden which supplies fresh produce for the table.

Simplicity

CONRAN'S LOVE OF SIMPLICITY in design is deep-rooted. 'I remember being taken as a child to visit Montacute House in Somerset. There were wonderful pictures on damask backdrops and carved and gilded furniture upstairs in the public rooms, but it was what was "below stairs" in the service rooms that really interested me. I found the shapes, forms and textures in the dairy aesthetically much more appealing.' This instinctive preference may have been partially influenced by his mother's taste – for 'big blocky cream linen loose covers on the sofa and chairs, and a plain beige carpet,' as Conran remembers. Then there was also the influence of his schooldays – Bryanston was a bracing, if not austere environment, where the strong sense of social purpose was reinforced by a rigorous regime of 'long runs and cold baths'. But his liking for the simple also has an economic rationale: 'I've always wanted to put in front of people things which look good but are inexpensive to make and buy.'

Simplicity is not necessarily simple to achieve. 'It's actually easier to do something very complicated and to make it look superficially luxurious. If you leave something undecorated, the shape matters more.' For early modernists, rejection of ornament and decoration amounted to a moral crusade; for minimalists, 'less is more' represents an almost spiritual quest for a beatific Zen calm. Conran's basic dislike of clutter and elaboration is more of an emotional response. 'Simplicity for me means allowing space for things to be looked at in depth. I find it very distracting in rooms where everything is so complicated you can't focus on anything.' For Conran, the absolute purity of minimalism lacks human warmth, and while he finds rooms bursting with possessions and rampant with pattern overwhelming and indigestible, he would never argue that they were in any sense 'wrong'.

He is predictably scathing about designs that reproduce past styles in an essentially meaningless way. Any form of pastiche, or ersatz luxury, he finds particularly abhorrent: mock Victorian coach lamps, mock Georgian doors, plasticized wood fascia in cars, fiddly mock Edwardian mouldings on kitchen cupboards, coy patterns of wheatsheaves embellishing toasters – for him such products peddle a basic untruth and obscure the essential beauty of many ordinary everyday things. One of Conran's long-running campaigns has been to direct attention towards the value of basic

SIMPLE OBJECTS
Personal selection

A few of Conran's favourite things (*opposite, clockwise from bottom right*): Japanese lacquerware, 3B pencil, watercolour paints, plumber's tool for beating and shaping lead pipes, ball of string, basketwork, milk bottle.

BLUE PRINT CAFÉ
Butlers Wharf, opened 1989

Simplicity and clarity is evident in the design of this restaurant, with its portholes revealing kitchen activity, its long upholstered banquette seating and its graphic blue and red colour scheme. Framed photographs are from the architecture and design magazine *Blueprint*.

objects, designs as familiar as the milk bottle or the paper clip whose simple forms can nevertheless represent an elegant design solution. 'People often forget that everything ever made by man or woman has been designed,' he points out. In the early 1970s he launched a Habitat range of plain no-nonsense household goods – called, appropriately enough, Basics – and later revisited the same idea with a new basic range in the early 1980s (later taken up by the company Muji, with shops all over the world).

Conran is aware that in many instances simplicity is actually much more practical. 'The Aeron chair produced by Herman Miller is a very clever piece of design. But it looks unattractive because it constantly gets dusty – there are just so many individual bits that dust can settle on and the cleaners can never get at.'

Simplicity in design can also be expressed in the clarity of planning or functional logic, a basic modernist approach to spatial design. 'First and foremost, my house books try to get people to look at the essentials – division of space, quality of light, proportion, heating, plumbing, and so on. I don't think it's possible to design a home successfully unless you know something about its infrastructure.' Planning a restaurant kitchen is an even greater challenge: with extremes of temperature, high levels of activity involving sharp implements and incredible pressure to produce the goods at a moment's notice, unnecessary complication can rapidly spell complete breakdown. 'In any restaurant kitchen, you need to ensure that work areas are clearly defined, that staff can do their job in quite a small space without getting in each other's way, and that everything's kept clean and tidy.'

When it comes to food, Conran is a natural advocate of Elizabeth David's maxim, *'Faites simple'*: 'Interior design and food nowadays show the same trend for simplicity. With food, it's fresh, good quality ingredients, simply cooked to

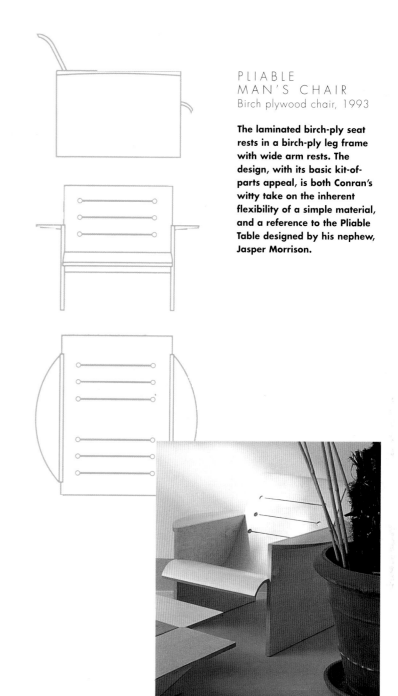

PLIABLE MAN'S CHAIR
Birch plywood chair, 1993

The laminated birch-ply seat rests in a birch-ply leg frame with wide arm rests. The design, with its basic kit-of-parts appeal, is both Conran's witty take on the inherent flexibility of a simple material, and a reference to the Pliable Table designed by his nephew, Jasper Morrison.

CLOCKS
Conran Collection,
1997

**Timekeeping simplified.
Conran's particular
favourite is the 'Ghost'
design _(top left and
centre)_ in white or
aluminium –
clockwatching at its
most minimal.**

BULB
Pendant lamp, Conran
Collection, 1997

**Conran's mission to
persuade people of the
beauty of everyday
things is exemplified in
this light fitting based
on a very familiar
household object.**

CONRAN

HAVANA
Leather club chair,
Conran
Collection, 1997

The comfort of an old favourite: Conran's interpretation of the traditional club chair. Leather upholstery smells wonderful and, of course, ages sympathetically.

knows that the difference between comfort and discomfort can rest in 'incredibly small tolerances – it can be a few millimetres here or there, a couple of degrees extra in the angle of an arm or back'. Just as he would advise that spatial design should begin with the functional logic of the plan and be informed by the basic infrastructure of servicing, for Conran physical comfort takes its reference from ergonomics – the postures, dimensions and proportions of the body at rest or engaged in different activities. But this is only a starting point. In all his designs, the production of the prototype is a key stage in the process, the first opportunity for what has been conceived as a drawing or model to be tested in the flesh. 'When a sample sofa comes in, for instance, we invite different people around the office to come and sit on it, lounge on it and tell us what they think.'

In a similar way, comfort is about finesse. This can be a visual finesse, where junctions between finishes and surfaces are well-detailed, or a sensual one which resides in material quality or workmanship. It can be the level of care that takes pains over finishing touches: buttoned fastenings on duvet covers, for example, or rolled edges on glassware; or the generosity expressed by thick bath towels, some chunky tumblers, big plates or fresh flowers massed in simple containers. In a retail environment, this sense of ease is conveyed both by visual plenty – the massing of goods – and by clever juxtapositions of products. 'The way in which a shop is laid out has enormous importance,' says Conran. 'We once moved the candles from one corner of the Conran Shop to another and it made a dramatic difference to sales. Selling china next to glass next to tableware next to table linen is about building associations, nudging and reminding the customer of how things work together. You also have to achieve a balance between stability and excitement, keeping the continuity but changing the face of the shop in small ways to generate a sense of anticipation.'

BLUEBIRD
CLUB
Opened 1997

Updating the notion of the private members' club, the warm, hospitable atmosphere relies on an evocative combination: the use of natural materials and the lively display of memorabilia recalling the career of British speed ace Malcolm Campbell. Car parts 'burn' in the gas flames.

43

Conveying this sense of ease in a restaurant involves a complex interrelation of factors. Lighting, for example, is a key element. At Quaglino's, which actually occupies a basement level with no direct natural light, the glazed ceiling is artificially backlit, with a state-of-the-art system of artificial lighting that varies subtly in level and intensity according to the time of day, ranging from the untroubled blue of midday to a deep midnight hue. By replicating natural conditions and rhythms, this helps to provide an instinctively more comfortable atmosphere for dining. At Butlers Wharf Chop House, the use of naturally finished timber for seating bays, partitions and flooring establishes a 'clubable' mood to accompany the hearty English cooking which is the restaurant's staple fare: here is true 'comfort' food in the best sense of the term, food – such as steak and kidney pudding – that is both warming and filling. Meanwhile, Le Pont de la Tour, with its long low horizontal lines, suggests the leisurely indulgence of the cruise liner crossed with the sophisticated intimacy of a 1940s' piano bar: comfort in this sense is simply having enough time to linger.

While Conran's work displays an integral consistency of approach, he is the last person to insist that everyone should toe the same stylistic line. 'I would find it incredibly depressing if someone furnished their entire home with what they had bought in a Conran Shop. What has always interested me is individual expression, whether it is precisely my taste or not.' When he first came to live in London, Conran used to walk down the streets and peer through lighted windows, intrigued by domestic tableaux that displayed different ways of furnishing and arranging what were basically very similar spaces. What attracted him most were confident displays of personality, rather than the predictable, safe or expected: the instinctive emotional comfort of knowing what one really likes.

STEAK AND KIDNEY PUDDING

Recipe courtesy David Hollis, chef at Butlers Wharf Chop House

INGREDIENTS (4 portions)

Pastry

- ❖ 250 g suet
- ❖ 500 g plain flour
- ❖ 1 dessertspoon salt
- ❖ 1 dessertspoon baking powder
- ❖ water to mix

Filling

- ❖ 1 kg stewing steak, diced (chuck steak is ideal)
- ❖ 1 ox kidney, diced
- ❖ 1 medium onion, finely diced
- ❖ 1 bay leaf
- ❖ salt, pepper and flour for dusting
- ❖ 1 400 ml can of Guinness
- ❖ 4 tablespoons Worcestershire sauce
- ❖ 500 ml veal stock made from veal bones

METHOD

Mix the pastry ingredients by hand, adding water to make a soft but workable dough. Cover with cling film and refrigerate.

Season and flour the steak and fry in a little oil until brown. Drain all fat from the pan, add the onion and bay leaf and continue frying for a further 2–3 minutes. Transfer to a large saucepan, add the Guinness, Worcestershire sauce and veal stock, then bring to the boil and simmer until the meat is nearly tender.

Meanwhile, place the kidneys in a pan of cold water and bring slowly to the boil, skimming off any impurities. When the water boils, remove from the heat and run the kidneys under cold water until cooled and any remaining impurities are gone. Add to the steak mixture and cook for a further 25–30 minutes. Season to taste with salt, pepper and Worcestershire sauce. Leave to cool.

Line four 1 pint pudding basins with cling film, roll the pastry to approx. 5 mm thick and line the basins with the pastry, reserving some for the lids.

Fill the basins to the top with the steak mixture, reserving some of the liquid. Cover each with a disc of pastry, crimping the edges together. Cover each pudding basin with a double layer of cling film and steam for 1 hour 20 minutes.

To serve, turn onto plates and pour over the remaining cooking liquor which has been strained through a muslin cloth. If you like oysters with your pudding, prior to serving poach briefly in the hot sauce and place on top of the puddings. Finish by sprinkling with chopped chives or parsley.

BUTLERS WHARF
CHOP HOUSE
Butlers Wharf,
opened 1993

Seating bays and flooring in naturally finished timber *(opposite)* emphasize the 'clubbable' atmosphere of this restaurant, which serves traditionally hearty dishes such as steak and kidney pudding.

ONRAN CAN TAKE SOME CREDIT for the fact that the British are now a little less readily shocked by the new – and can sometimes even be persuaded to like it. He has, perhaps, proved that there is an acceptable face of modernity, that it can be employed in a human way. 'I'm not a believer in modernity for modernity's sake,' he says, 'but I like to think I'm sufficiently rational to want to live in the world as it is today, rather than hark back to the past which so many see as a soft option. I have always found it strange that people seem so keen on modernity in some areas of their lives and so resistant to it in others. They may take great pride in owning a hi-tech computer or stereo, but carry on decorating their homes as if it were a hundred years ago. There might be a brand new car sitting in the drive, but the house has a fake Georgian door and coach lamps.'

Conran's belief in the basic tenets of modernism, and his conviction that design has the power to improve the quality of life for everyone, dates back to his student days at Central, when he was first exposed to the ideals of the Bauhaus. Design there was taught along similar lines to those first laid down at that birthplace of European modernism; indeed, some of the Central teachers had themselves been taught by Bauhaus members. Conran owes his egalitarian views to this period of his life, and he has stuck by them ever since.

Notable among successful entrepreneurs for putting his money where his mouth is, Conran established the charitable Conran Foundation, dedicated to promoting design education in Britain, 'as soon as Habitat was floated on the public exchange and I found myself with some proper money'. The Boilerhouse project, which

DESIGN MUSEUM
Butlers Wharf,
opened 1989

Housed in a converted 1950s warehouse, completely renovated and redesigned by Conran Architects, the Design Museum is the only permanent collection of modern design in Britain.

opened at the Victoria and Albert Museum in 1981, was funded by the Foundation and designed by Conran Associates who transformed 460 square metres (5,000 square feet) of derelict space in the boilerhouse yard on the west of the museum into a pure white modernist space. Its first exhibition, *Art and Industry: A century of design in the products you use,* reflected the campaigning aims of the Foundation – to bring a new awareness of the importance of design to both the public at large and British industry. Five years of hugely successful exhibitions followed.

In 1989, three years after the Boilerhouse closed, the Design Museum opened at Butlers Wharf. 'Achieving the Design Museum was a moment of real pleasure,' says Conran, but it was not without its moments of controversy. The Museum was housed in a converted 1950s

DESIGN MUSEUM
Butlers Wharf, opened 1989

An important annual event is the Conran Foundation's selection of new work, chosen every year by a different figure from the world of design. The 1997 collection (above) was selected by garden designer Dan Pearson.

The renovation of an old department store provided the exciting opportunity to create a modern retail environment.

warehouse, stripped down to its steel structure and completely renovated and redesigned by Conran Architects. At model stage, the design was shown to the Prince of Wales, who did not like it. 'I made a little speech arguing the merits of the design and the value of a modern approach,' says Conran. 'At the end, I said that surely he wouldn't want to be remembered as Charles III, the Repro Monarch.'

The Design Museum and its exhibitions represent a persuasive argument for the value of design in modern society. 'One of the reasons I became a businessman was to be in a position to remove some of the prejudice against design and to be able to demonstrate, in a language that accountants would understand, that aesthetics can be just as important as engineering – indeed the two should go hand in hand. There is this notion that design is an optional extra, something that costs more but ultimately isn't worth it. But if a designer improves how a product works or enhances our enjoyment of it, then design must be value added.' It is not a view that has always received a favourable reception, either in British industry or among government circles. Like many arts and cultural institutions in Britain today, the Design Museum survives largely by attracting corporate sponsorship, such as the recent funding by Gucci of an exhibition on Charles and Ray Eames. 'It's important that we raise people's awareness, understanding and appreciation of architecture and design, so that the public comes to see that they are not alien or threatening but rather can help us engage with and negotiate the world around us. In the best examples, modernity is extremely exciting.'

'I'm interested in modernity only if it leads to something better,' says Conran. This philosophy of improvement does not necessarily mean razing the old to make way for the new, but often entails renovation of what already exists. From Butlers Wharf and Bluebird to the Miche-

GEORGE'S
Department store,
Melbourne,
opened 1998

Old buildings, particularly those with strong architectural character, lend themselves to new uses. For Conran, modernity does not necessarily mean getting rid of the old.

MEZZONINE
Soho, opened 1995

Upstairs from Mezzo, Mezzonine represents an updating of the worker's canteen, its rigorous modern aesthetic in keeping with the Far Eastern-inspired menu of high quality fast food.

lin Building, from the new Melbourne Conran Shop (which is part of the redevelopment of an old department store) to the siting of the Hamburg Conran Shop in the regenerated docklands district, the adaptation of perfectly serviceable surroundings to new uses is one example of Conran's balanced take on modernism. 'Warehouses and disused industrial buildings often provide a subtle palette of colours and textures, such as exposed brickwork, joists and pipes, wooden or stone floors,' he says. ' I would hate to see a conversion which covered up these features, but at the same time, you don't want an interior stripped of comfort. Minimalist rooms are no more honest than a newly built house kitted out with pastiche Victoriana.'

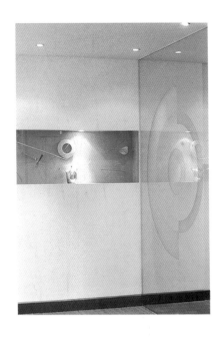

ENTRANCE
DISPLAY
Conran Collection shop,
Conduit Street,
opened 1998

The internal window in the entrance to the Conran Collection shop provides a focal point for display, with products artfully lit by recessed halogen downlighters. 'Modern living made simple' is the rationale behind the launch of this range.

CONRAN
COLLECTION
SHOP
Conduit Street,
opened 1998

A feature of this
striking contemporary
shop is the distinctive
yet versatile fittings
which were specially
designed to display
the products in the
collection. The fittings
can be adapted to a
variety of sites when
further shops open.

OWN LABEL
FOOD
Conran Collection, 1997

Conran's extensive experience in the field of identity has made him particularly sensitive to the use of design in the enhancement of image. Strong colours, clear graphics and good quality packaging are a feature of all his work in this area.

MURAL
Cantina del Ponte,
Butlers Wharf, 1992

In the context of restaurant design, identity can mean creating a sense of place or destination. This mural by artist Timna Woollard, which occupies the end wall of Cantina del Ponte at Butlers Wharf, depicts an Italian market scene, in keeping with the restaurant's simple Italian fare.

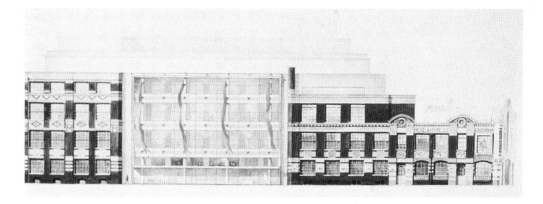

BIBENDUM
Michelin Building, 1987

The tyre company's rotund mascot provides a point of reference for Bibendum, located in the renovated Michelin Building. Since its launch, Bibendum has been consistently rated one of London's top restaurants.

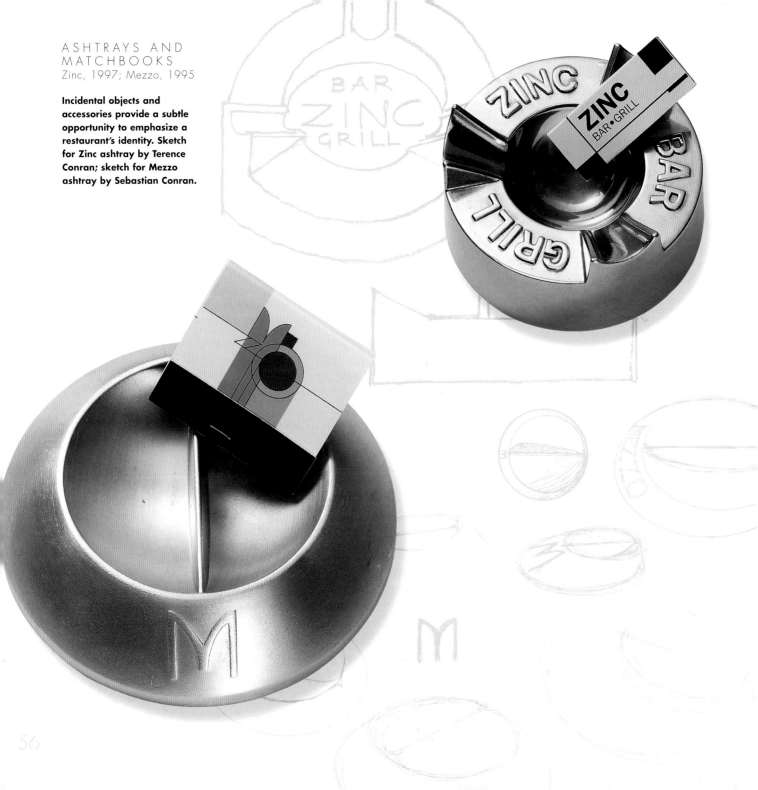

ASHTRAYS AND MATCHBOOKS
Zinc, 1997; Mezzo, 1995

Incidental objects and accessories provide a subtle opportunity to emphasize a restaurant's identity. Sketch for Zinc ashtray by Terence Conran; sketch for Mezzo ashtray by Sebastian Conran.

ZINC
BAR·GRILL

ZINC
BAR·GRILL

there's little point building the image to start with. When we took over British Home Stores, for example, it was obvious that a major jolt was required. The decision not to ditch the original name was crucial. People don't want to see a brand completely obliterated unless it is wrong or corrupt.'

The focus of identity is the logo or trademark. 'Some of the most successful brands – such as Shell – only need fine tuning, little adjustments over the years. But I think most people find it difficult to remember purely visual logos. If you asked someone to draw the ICI symbol, for example, I doubt that they could do it. There's also a tendency for abstract symbols to over-intellectualize the issue. The success of the Habitat logo came from having a good name to start with and putting it together with the lower-case type style that was right for its time.'

In retail, packaging is obviously an important means of conveying image and identity. 'Packaging, like branding, is what gets between the product and the customer. I think that packag-ing should be totally subservient to the product or there's built-in disappointment. Similarly, you can take branding too far to the extent that the diversity of what is on offer in the shop is no longer apparent, as everything looks the same.'

Practicality matters, but so does enjoyment. 'For a shop like Habitat, where much of the furniture was flat-pack, packaging was vital as a means of protection. But in other contexts, it is also a way of creating a sense of anticipation – the enjoyment of opening a box, of unfolding the tissue, transfers to the product. At the Conran Shop, our paper bags are quite expensive to produce – far more expensive than plastic would be – and I have had quite a lot of pressure over the years to reduce the cost, which I have resisted. Cheap plastic can be depressing and offers very little protection, whereas a good quality bag with bright, cheerful graphics provides a sense of pleasure as you walk out of the shop.'

ASHTRAYS AND MATCHBOOKS
Bluebird Club, 1997;
Sartoria, 1998

The number on the Bluebird matchbook is Malcolm Campbell's 1934 land speed record: 301.129 mph. The Sartoria ashtray takes the form of a tailor's coiled tape measure.

57

CARRIER BAGS
Conran Collection and Conran
Shop, 1998

**Good quality packaging matters
to Conran, whose shop bags have
always been made of paper
rather than flimsy polythene and
designed with care, just like any
other product.**

As is the case with much of Conran's work, in the area of image-building he often has what he calls an 'unfair advantage', since he and his designers are effectively designing for their own use rather than an outside client. 'I like to put some charm and humour into my projects. In the restaurants, incidental items such as cruets and ashtrays, menus and graphics provide the opportunity to express a sense of personality. The Quaglino's ashtray is iconic – and obviously covetable since so many people steal them. The ashtray we designed for Sartoria, in the form of a curled tape measure, together with the use of tailor's tools on the graphic side, is intended both as a gentle acknowledgement of the tailoring tradition of the area where the restaurant is located, and a counterpoint to the Italian food and wine it serves. But it is also the sort of thing that gets me accused of making a "theme" restaurant!'

Habitat, one of the first 'lifestyle' stores, was an early example of the retailer as brand rather than a stocker of brands. Its significance can be gauged from the fact that years after its opening, people still tend to remember their first purchase – whether it was a pine table, a duvet, a chicken brick or a set of enamelled saucepans. Since the Habitat days, Conran has increasingly found himself in the enviable position of having a name that is itself an identity, that has come to stand for the qualities of design and the attitudes to living which he has spent a lifetime trying to promote. 'I recently took one of the directors of L'Oréal on a quick tour of some London shops,' Conran recalls. 'We visited Paul Smith, Sartoria, Bluebird and the Conran Collection shop in Conduit Street. He was surprised by how much more personal and individual shopping was here, compared to France, and said that in each case one could tell that there was someone behind it all who really cared.'

Conran Shop Christmas
catalogue, 1997;
Bluebird Christmas
broadsheet, 1997

Lively, colourful and clearly laid out, catalogues and information sheets are not only powerful selling tools but also a means of reinforcing the Conran identity across a wide range of endeavours. Conran himself proudly displays his wares for the Conran Shop Christmas catalogue *(opposite)*.

Chronology

1931
Terence Conran born in Esher, Surrey.

1946–48
Attends Bryanston School, Dorset.

1948–50
Studies textile design at the Central School of Arts and Crafts in London.

1952
Sets up own furniture-making business selling primarily to the contracts market. As the business expands, company moves to Thetford, Norfolk.

1953
Visits France for the first time; on return to London opens his first restaurant, the Soup Kitchen in Chandos Place.

1954
Opens The Orrery restaurant, in King's Road.

1956
Founds Conran Design Group (CDG), initially as an ancillary business to the furniture-making group. Over the next 35 years, CDG grows to become one of the largest design consultancies in Europe, handling retail, office, product and graphic design projects worldwide.

1964
Opens the first Habitat, in Fulham Road.

1968
Merges with stationers to become Ryman Conran.

1970
Buys out Habitat from Ryman Conran.

1971
Opens the Neal Street Restaurant in Covent Garden (now run by his brother-in-law, Antonio Carluccio).

1973
Opens the first Conran Shop, in Fulham Road.

1980
Founds architects and town planning company Conran Roche. The company goes on to design many high-profile buildings including London's Design Museum and the Michelin Building redevelopment.

1981
Establishes The Conran Foundation, a charitable fund dedicated to educating schoolchildren, the public and British industry on the values of industrial design.

1982
Takes over Mothercare after floating Habitat on the stock exchange in October 1981. The following year the Habitat/Mothercare group takes over Heal's and womenswear chain Richard Shops.

1983
Habitat/Mothercare embarks on joint publishing venture with Octopus Books, under the name Conran Octopus (later bought by Reed International). Terence Conran is awarded a knighthood in the Queen's New Year Honours.

1985
Sets up Benchmark Woodworking, with Sean Sutcliffe, making furniture for Conran's restaurants and for sale through Conran Shops.

1986
Habitat/Mothercare merges with British Home Stores to create Storehouse plc, with Terence Conran as chairman and chief executive.

1987
Opens Bibendum restaurant in the renovated Michelin Building, Fulham Road.

1989
The Design Museum opens at Butlers Wharf, London, funded by the Conran Foundation. Opens the Blue Print Café on the first floor. Receives the D&AD President's Award for outstanding contribution to British Design.

1990
Terence Conran retires as chairman of Storehouse plc (having retired as chief executive the previous year) and buys back The Conran Shop. CDG is bought from Storehouse by the French-owned communications group RSCG. Terence Conran becomes joint president of RSCG's international design division (retires 1992).

1991
Opens Le Pont de la Tour restaurant in Butlers Wharf.

1992
Opens Cantina del Ponte restaurant in Butlers Wharf. Opens the first Conran Shop in Paris.

1993
Opens Quaglino's restaurant and Butlers Wharf Chop House. Forms CD Partnership. Projects include the Bluebird Foodmarket and Restaurant; The Conran Shop, Marylebone Road; and Hotel Das Triest, Vienna. Ongoing work includes several new Conran Shops and restaurant

projects in London, Paris and New York.

1994
Opens The Conran Shop in Tokyo.

1995
Opens Mezzo restaurant in Soho.

1996
Opens The Conran Shop in Hamburg.

1997
Opens Bluebird restaurant and shop; Zinc Bar & Grill; Orrery restaurant; and The Conran Shop.

1998
Opens Sartoria restaurant; Coq d'Argent; and Alcazar restaurant and bar in Paris. Opens The Conran Shop in Melbourne, Australia, and the first Conran Collection shop in London's Conduit Street.

1999
Opens a second Conran Shop in Paris. Work continues on Bridgemarket development in Manhattan and Great Eastern Hotel in London, both of which are scheduled to open autumn 1999.

Index

Acknowledgements

The publishers wish to thank Terence Conran, Simon Willis and Jamie Abbott at Conran Ltd for their kind assistance with all aspects of this book. Additional thanks to the Bluebird Kitchen Shop for supplying the kitchen tools illustrated on pages 14 and 15.

Photographic credits

Bibendum Restaurant: pages 55 right, 61 left.

CD Partnership: pages 48, 49 above.

Stafford Cliff and David Brittain: pages 9, 26 left, 37.

The Conran Collection (photographs by Earl Carter, James Merrell, Robin Rout, Diana Miller, Georgia Glyn Smith): pages 17, 22, 23, 26 below, 38, 39, 40, 41, 42, 50, 51, 54 right, 60 right.

Conran Octopus: page 28.

Conran Restaurants (photographs by Mark Lawrence, Helen Drew, Stafford Cliff, David Brittain, James Murphy, Georgia Glyn Smith, Anne Soderberg, Jonathan Pile): pages 6, 8, 10, 24, 25, 26 above, 27, 30, 31, 36, 43, 44, 45, 49 below, 52, 53, 54 left, 55 below, 59 below, 61 below.

The Conran Shop (photographs by Jonathan Pile, James Merrell, Robin Rout): pages 32, 55 above, 58 above, 59 above left and right.

Country Life (photographs by Craig Knowles): pages 20, 21.

Design Museum (photographs Peter Cook, Jefferson Smith): pages 46, 47, 60 below.

Habitat: pages 11, 60 above.

Andrew Lawson: page 33.

Mitchell Beazley (publishers): page 29 (photograph shown in bottom spread © Knoll International).

Guy Ryecart: pages 5, 14, 15, 18, 34, 35, 54, 55, 58 below.

BROOKLANDS COLLEGE LIBRARY
WEYBRIDGE, SURREY KT13 8TT